SO YOU THINK YOU KNOW?

DUNDEE

Produced by The Francis Frith Collection
exclusively for

OTTAKAR'S

www.ottakars.co.uk

First published in the United Kingdom in 2005 by The Francis Frith Collection®

Hardback edition published in 2005 ISBN 1-84567-799-4

Text and Design copyright The Francis Frith Collection®
Photographs copyright The Francis Frith Collection® except where indicated.

British Library Cataloguing in Publication Data

So You Think You Know? Dundee
Text adapted from original material supplied by Gillian Nicole Ferguson

The Francis Frith Collection
Frith's Barn, Teffont,
Salisbury, Wiltshire SP3 5QP
Tel: +44 (0) 1722 716 376
Email: info@francisfrith.co.uk
www.francisfrith.co.uk

Printed and bound in England

Front Cover: **DUNDEE, THE ALEXANDRA FOUNTAIN 1907** D81001t

The colour-tinting is for illustrative purposes only, and is not intended to be historically accurate

CONTENTS

DUNDEE MISCELLANY

The name 'Dundee' is thought to have come from the Celtic 'duntaw' (hill on the Tay), or possibly from the Iron Age fort which was located on the top of the Law and was called Dun Diagh.

Dundee's Law is all that remains of an extinct volcano.

William Wallace attended the Grammar School in Dundee's High Street as a young man. A fight with a fellow pupil, Selbie, ended in murder when Wallace stabbed him. Unfortunately for Wallace, Selbie was the son of an English governor, and Wallace was forced to flee the town.

It cost just over £5 to hang and burn a witch in Dundee. Records from 1590 give details of the cost which included the transporting of the wretched accused, the purchasing of coal, tar and rope, and the payment for the hangman.

The shoreline in Dundee was originally much higher; it ran just in front of the Seagate and along the bottom of Castle Street.

3

Mass graves thought to contain the remains of those killed during the massacre by General Monck's troops in 1651 have been found around St Mary's Church on three separate occasions: during the laying of tram tracks in the 19th century, whilst the Old Overgate was being demolished in the 1960s, and more recently when landscaping was being undertaken around the churches.

General Monck's House, at the entrance of the Overgate, with its unusual circular corner tower was for centuries an early tourist attraction in Dundee. It survived until the 1960s, when it was demolished to make way for the new shopping centre.

In the archives at Dundee University, a piece of sailcloth from Nelson's 'Victory' survives. The sails from important ships were often cut up to make souvenirs, but this piece is particularly interesting, as it bears the maker's stamp, Baxter Bros from Dundee!

In the 1820s, the Dundee & Newtyle railway line builders faced a particularly difficult problem of how to navigate the Law. Their solution was to create a quarter-mile-long tunnel through the eastern flank of the hill.

DUNDEE, CASTLE COURT c1870 SA000134
(Courtesy of University of St Andrews Library)

DUNDEE, HIGH STREET FROM THE WEST 1887 SA000113
(Courtesy of University of St Andrews Library)

The poet William Topaz McGonagall (1825-1902), universally regarded as one of the worst poets ever, made Dundee his adopted home. The self-educated loom weaver claimed that the Goddess of Poetry visited him in Paton's Lane in 1877, and he once walked the fifty miles to Balmoral to visit Queen Victoria. After being stopped at the gate he was told never to come back.

The postage stamp was first suggested by a Dundee bookseller, James Chalmers, in 1822 (a full year before Sir Rowland Hill was officially credited with its invention). Chalmers's idea of a low-cost postage stamp was the basis of our present mailing system. Chalmers died in 1853 aged 71, and his gravestone can be found in Dundee's Howff.

One of the first doctors to use X-ray technology was Dr George Alexander Pirie, who first began using X-rays at Dundee's Royal Infirmary in 1896.

A few months before the Wright Brothers, Preston Watson achieved powered flight in Dundee with his 'wiggle-waggle' flying machine.

James Bowman Lindsay, who lived in Dundee, was one of the first to develop electric light in the 19th century.

DUNDEE, THE ADMIRAL'S TREE, CAMPERDOWN HOUSE 1880 SA000155
(Courtesy of University of St Andrews Library)

In the 1950s, Dundee played host to a number of famous performers such as Bob Hope, Danny Kaye, Mario Lanza and Frank Sinatra (only 600 tickets were sold for his first night). In the 1960s both the Beatles and the Rolling Stones played at Caird Hall.

The first female trade union leader in Britain was Margaret Fenwick in Dundee.

Dundee has featured in a number of films over the years. In 1983 the Caird Hall stood in for the Bolshoi Theatre in 'An Englishman Abroad'. In 1988, the High School played the part of the Berlin Reichstag and the then dilapidated Camperdown Works played the role of bombed Berlin in 'Christabel', scripted by Dennis Potter. More recently, Dundee played itself in the BBC's 'Jute City', a detective story set in the city.

Aspirin was developed by Dr Thomas John MacLagan in 1876 whilst he worked at Dundee's Royal Infirmary.

The Mills Observatory, located at the top of Balgay Hill, is the only full-time public observatory still in use. It is hard to believe, but the dome was originally made of papier mache.

Dundee was voted the 'Friendliest Campus in Scotland', according to the 'Virgin Guide to British Universities'.

The Dundee Blues Bonanza, held every July in the city, is the biggest in Europe. For three days hundreds of musicians and fans descend on the city to celebrate the music that they love.

The Dundee Book Prize was first established in 2000 and attracted 82 entries. Run in conjunction by the City of Discovery Campaign and the University of Dundee, the £6000 prize also includes the publication of the winning novel; although novels on any theme and of any genre can be entered, the first two winners both chose to set their novels in the city.

The statue of a dragon located in the city centre comes from a local legend. A farmer from Pitempton lost all nine of his beautiful young daughters to a hungry dragon. A bold lad, Martin, who had loved the farmer's eldest daughter, pledged to rid the countryside of the beast and avenge his lost love. Martin attacked the beast and killed it, and the spot where it fell is marked with the Pictish Martin's Stone.

Dundee's Nine Incorporated Trades were formed in the 16th century so that they might receive a fair price for their services, and to discourage non-members from undercutting the price of their goods. The nine members, which were listed in order of importance, were the bakers, the cordiners (shoemakers), the glovers, the tailors, the bonnet makers, the fleshers (butchers), the hammermen (metal workers), the weavers, and the dyers. One of their earliest meeting places was within the Howff cemetery. Each trade held its meeting at the gravestone of one of its former members

Dundee City Churches in the Nethergate was for many years the longest church in Europe, and today is still the largest non-cathedral church in Scotland.

DUNDEE, THE ROYAL INFIRMARY 1878 SA000115
(Courtesy of University of St Andrews Library)

DUNDEE, WISHART ARCH 1878 SA000132
(Courtesy of University of St Andrews Library)

For centuries there has been the belief that the treasure which General Monck's armies looted from Dundee is still on the seabed somewhere between Broughty Castle and Tayport. Although the water is only around 40ft deep in this area, the sandbanks and currents are notoriously treacherous. If the haul included 200,000 gold coins as some believe, along with other precious items, it could be worth over £2 billion in today's money.

Dundee has always been an important centre for whaling. The Dundee Whale Fishing Company was set up in 1754. By 1811 the whaling fleet consisted of ten ships, and was big enough to rival Peterhead. With the introduction of coal gas lighting the industry began to suffer, as whale oil was no longer required to light lamps. The industry was saved as Dundee's use of jute grew: whale oil was vital to soften the raw jute.

On 11 May 1797, Admiral Duncan encountered the Dutch fleet off the coast near the village of Camperdown. The battle that followed lasted for five hours, but the Dutch eventually surrendered to Admiral Duncan. Duncan was

hailed a hero and given the title of Viscount Duncan of Camperdown. On his return to Dundee the name of the family estate was changed from Lundie to Camperdown, and his portrait was placed in the Town Hall.

DUNDEE, THE ALEXANDRA FOUNTAIN 1907 D81001

DUNDEE, HIGH STREET c1903 SA000149
(Courtesy of University of St Andrews Library)

Captain Robert Falcon Scott, or 'Scott of the Antarctic', became a national hero when he completed his National Antarctic Expedition of 1901-04. Dundee shipbuilders built his ship, the RRS 'Discovery', especially for the expedition; through their experience of building whaling ships, they were able to provide Scott with a vessel that could withstand the demanding journey.

One of the worst disasters to affect the city was the collapse of the rail bridge in December 1879. The bridge was opened in May 1878; at over two miles long it was the longest bridge in the world. On the evening of 28 December 1879 the bridge collapsed during a storm while a train was crossing, and seventy-five people fell to their death. The piers of the original bridge can still be seen in the river.

Dundee's last execution by hanging was carried out on 24 April 1889. William Henry Bury strangled his wife, stabbed her viciously, and then kept her body in a box (which his friends unknowingly played cards upon) for several days before confessing to the crime.

The Keillor family business began when a Mrs Keillor invented a new recipe for marmalade after receiving a batch of particularly bitter oranges. Her son, James, established the business, and the company began to produce jam as well as marmalade enjoyed all over the world.

D C Thomson's publishing company was established in 1905, after an amalgamation of two much older papers, and is still in business today. Among its many publications are the Dundee Courier and Evening Telegraph, and also the Beano, the Dandy, the Sunday Post and the People's Friend. Legend has it that the Bash Street Kids from the Beano were inspired by the artist Leo Baxendale's view of the children in the playground of the adjacent High School.

Dundee, despite its size, has two high-profile football teams: Dundee Football Club, founded in 1893 and located at Dens Park since 1919, and located across the road at Tannadice Park, Dundee United Football Club, dating from 1909. The Dundee Derby, when the two rivals play one another, is one of the most anticipated matches for the fans of both teams.

Hidden behind later buildings on the High Street, and accessed through Gray's Close, Gardyne's Land is the oldest residential building to survive in Dundee. The house was built for a prosperous merchant, and the building's sophistication is an indicator of Dundee's wealth and status at the time. It is currently being restored by the excellent Tayside Building Preservation Trust with plans to create a five-star backpackers' hostel, much needed in Dundee.

Opened in 1999, the Dundee Contemporary Arts centre (DCA) has attracted over 900,000 visitors since its opening. DCA has been successful in attracting several international artists' work to Dundee, and there is a strong focus on community activities. The centre includes five floors of galleries, a print centre, educational facilities and the University of Dundee visual research centre. Incorporated within the building is the Jute Cafe Bar, a busy restaurant and popular nightspot.

DUNDEE, WEST PARK ROAD 1935 SA000162
(Courtesy of University of St Andrews Library)

In December 1883 a humpback whale marooned on a sandbank in the Tay was harpooned and exhibited in Dock Street, much to the excitement of the locals. The skeleton of the whale can still be seen in the McManus Galleries.

In the late 19th and early 20th century, the Seagate was the location of numerous whisky bonds, including Watson's bond and Robertson's bond. In July 1906 a fire destroyed Watson's whisky bond and caused much damage to the street. The Dundee Yearbook from the period states that Seagate was turned into 'a river of burning whisky'!

The ship the 'Mars' was moored in the Tay from 1869 and was home to boys, many orphaned or delinquents, until it was broken up in 1929. Conditions on board were probably grim, but it was felt that the boys were given a better chance in life, as they were trained for a naval career. A spell on the 'Mars' was preferable to one in prison - in 1846 more than 100 children under the age of fourteen were sent to Dundee Jail.

Local legend tells of a young man who left Dundee a poor sailor and returned the captain of a fine ship. On entering the Tay he commented on the strange smell in the air, and was told that a witch was being burnt at the stake. On hearing her name, Grizzel Jaffrey, he ordered that the ship be turned around, and never returned to Dundee. Grizzel Jaffrey was his mother.

DUNDEE, HIGH STREET c1903 SA000149
(Courtesy of University of St Andrews Library)

William Dobson Valentine was a pioneer in underwater photography. In 1882, he published the results of his (unsuccessful) attempts to photograph the engine, tender and carriages on the bed of the Tay after the Tay Bridge disaster.

In 1991 Dundee celebrated its octocentenary with a year-long birthday party. Most memorable of the events was a summer carnival, and many remember the gasometer that was made to look like a giant birthday cake.

Dundee has long been associated with the three Js, jute, jam and journalism, the three industries that helped to build the city. The jute and jam industry have gone, and today only journalism survives within Dundee.

It is important to remember the unique role that women played within Dundee's jute industry. Dundee earned the name of 'She-Toon' because, unlike many other places at the time, so many women were employed within the factories. Society at the time felt that the woman's place was in the home. When a woman married she was often expected to give up work, yet in Dundee a large percentage of the workforce was not only female, but also married. It was often difficult for men to find permanent work within the mills, and many young boys would become unemployed upon completing their apprenticeships, as they would then have been entitled to adult male rates of pay. With women out at work, many of Dundee's families experienced a role reversal: the men became 'kettle-bilers' (kettle boilers), so called because they stayed at home to look after the household chores and children.

DUNDEE, WELLGATE STEPS c1911 SA000179
(Courtesy of University of St Andrews Library)

DUNDEE, OLD TOWER AND CROSS 1880 SA00014
(Courtesy of University of St Andrews Library)

Dundee has the tag 'Scotland's univerCity' and there are more students per head of population than anywhere else in Scotland.

As a symbol of Dundee's regaining confidence, the architect William Adam was employed to design the new Town House. Commonly known as 'the Pillars', and built in 1731, this impressive seven-bay building was thought to be one of the finest buildings in Scotland at the time. The ground floor of the building held an arcade of shops and a bank, while above was a court, a jail and the City Chambers. The building was demolished in 1932, but its name lives on in the Pillars Bar that still trades in Crichton Street, where a model of the Town House hangs above its entrance.

DUNDEE, AN OLD HOUSE IN CHURCH LANE, NETHERGATE 1878 SA000118
(Courtesy of University of St Andrews Library)

Dundonians have always loved going to the pictures, or the cinema, and in the 1930s the city had more cinema seats per head than anywhere else in Europe.

In 1908 Winston Churchill campaigned to become MP for Dundee despite several demonstrations from the suffragettes led by Emmeline Pankhurst. With such a high number of women workers, the Votes for Women campaign found strong support in Dundee. Churchill won his campaign, but later suffered a humiliating defeat in 1922 and vowed never to set foot in Dundee again - a vow he kept.

DUNDEE, THE FOOT OF BONNET HILL c1878 SA000136
(Courtesy of University of St Andrews Library)

DUNDEE, THE TIME GUN c1880 SA000186
(Courtesy of University of St Andrews Library)

Dundee's time gun was situated in the grounds of Dudhope Castle high above the city. Normally fired daily at 1pm, it was silenced in 1916 so as not to disturb shell-shocked soldiers recovering in Dundee Royal Infirmary.

Built in 1909, the King's Theatre was the most outstanding of Dundee's theatres. The auditorium was opulently decorated with gilded plaster mouldings and dark crimson upholstery. There was also a superb domed ceiling with frescoes. Marie Lloyd and Harry Lauder were just two of the famous names to play the King's. Today the King's still exists as a nightclub.

27

DUNDEE QUIZ QUESTIONS

1. Where does the name 'Dundee' come from?

2. What was the 'Rotten Row'?

3. When did Dundee become a royal burgh?

4. Which king's troops captured Broughty Castle in 1548?

5. What did Mary, Queen of Scots grant Dundee in 1564?

6. What happened to General Monk's ships in 1651 as they sailed out of Dundee?

7. What item of clothing was woven in the Hilltown?

8. What animal was caught in the Tay estuary in December 1883 (its skeleton is on display in the McManus Galleries)?

9. Where was Dundee's first official theatre?

10. What are the three Js?

DUNDEE, THE TAY BRIDGE FROM THE FIFE SIDE c1879 SA000105
(Courtesy of University of St Andrews Library)

11. Who designed the Albert Institute?

12. When did the Tay rail bridge collapse?

13. What was cut through the Law in the 1820s?

14. What is the name of the oldest floating warship, which is still docked in Dundee?

15. Which citizen of Dundee invented the postage stamp?

DUNDEE, HIGH STREET c1900 SA000193
(Courtesy of University of St Andrews Library)

16. Who was Grizzel Jaffrey?

17. What was the name of Preston Watson's flying machine?

18. In the 1988 TV series 'Christabel', what was the High School decorated to look like?

19. What are 'the Bakers, Cordiners, Glovers, Tailors, Bonnet makers, Fleshers, Hammermen, Weavers and Dyers' better known as?

20. In which year did Admiral Duncan fight the Dutch fleet at the Battle of Camperdown?

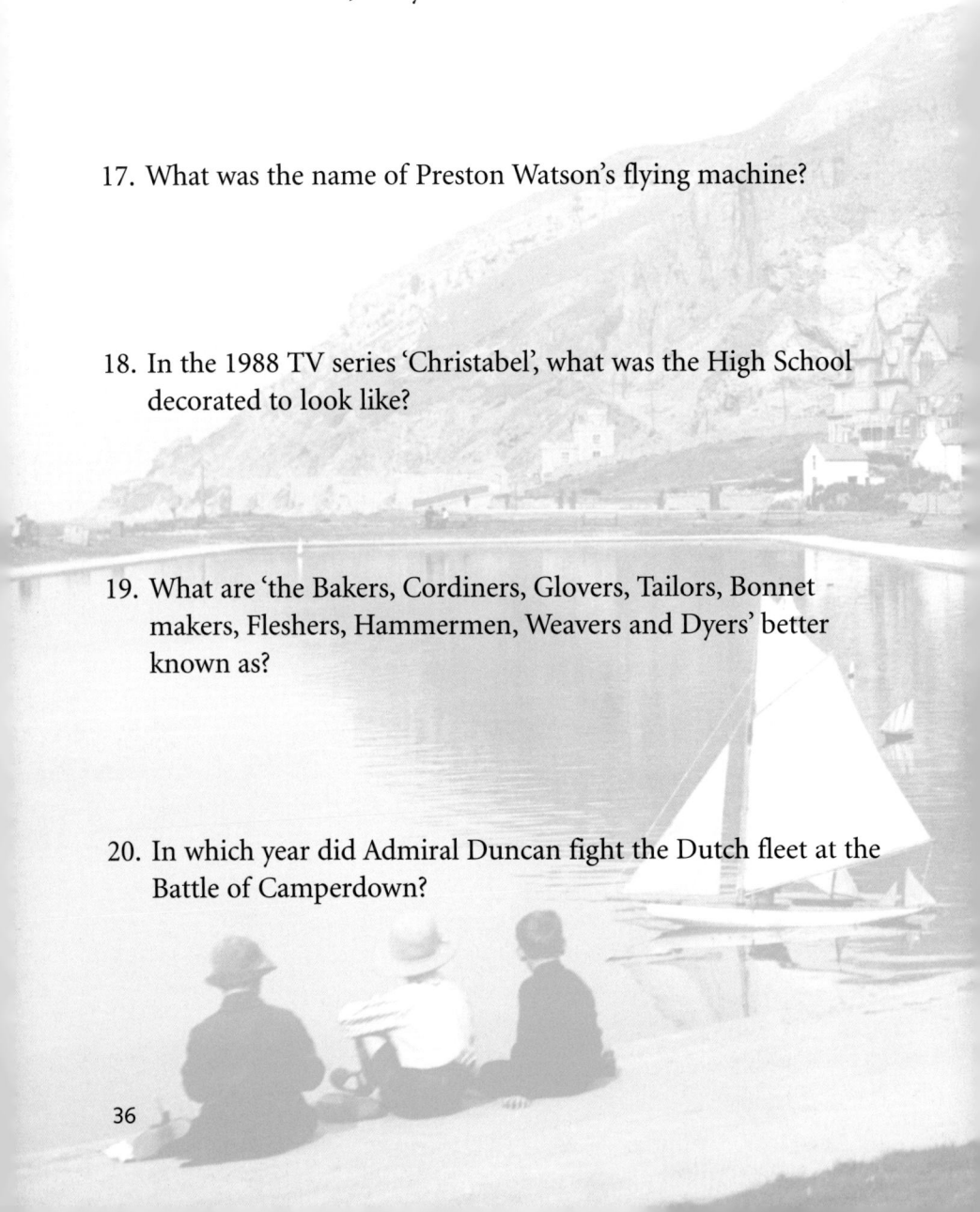

DUNDEE, MURRAYGATE 1934 SA000167
(Courtesy of University of St Andrews Library)

21. When was Dundee's last public hanging carried out?

22. Where, in the city centre, is Dundee's oldest residential building?

23. What flowed through the Seagate in July 1906?

24. What was moored in the Tay from 1869 to 1929?

25. What were the Keillors famous for?

26. Dundee had a special birthday in 1991. How old was the city?

27. Where could you see Dundee's main time gun?

DUNDEE, THE HEAD OF THE SEAGATE 1878 SA000117
(Courtesy of University of St Andrews Library)

DUNDEE, THE ROYAL ARCH 1878 SA000121
(Courtesy of University of St Andrews Library)

28. Which former prime minister was Liberal MP for Dundee
    between 1908 and 1922?

29. Name the comic 'cowboy' who can be seen striding through
    Dundee's city centre.

30. In Dundee, what was a 'half-timer'?

31. Which Dundee jute manufacturer made the sails used on
    Nelson's 'Victory'?

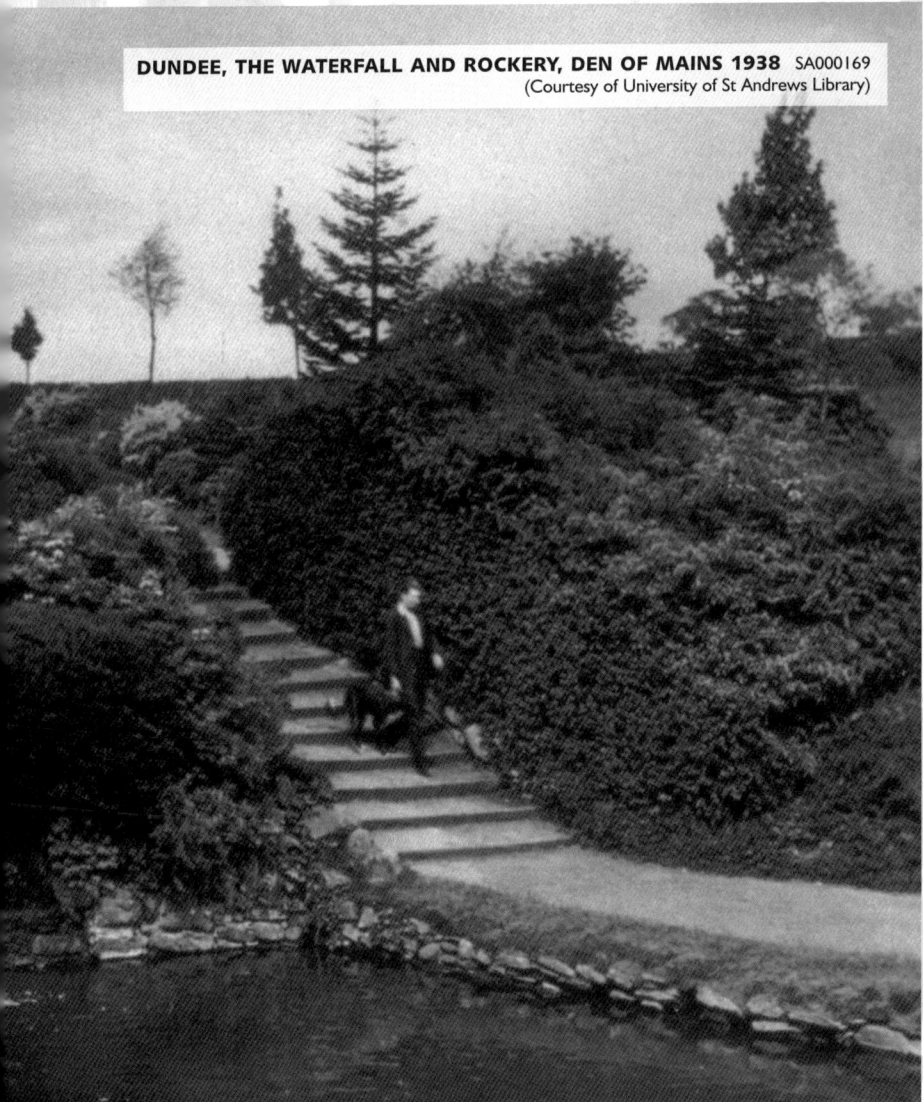

DUNDEE, THE WATERFALL AND ROCKERY, DEN OF MAINS 1938 SA000169
(Courtesy of University of St Andrews Library)

DUNDEE, THE NORTH GATE TO BALGAY PARK 1878 SA000144
(Courtesy of University of St Andrews Library)

32. What were Dundee's jute productions used for in the Wild West?

33. What kind of oil was used to soften raw jute fibres?

34. Name the tallest chimneystack still present in Dundee.

35. Can you name Dundee's new scientific research centre?

36. What is the name of Captain Scott's ship, which has returned home to Dundee?

37. Name the 'X-Men 2' star who was born in Dundee.

38. How high is the Law? 472 feet, 572 feet or 672 feet?

39. In the two world wars, which type of vessel commonly used Dundee's harbour as a base?

40. What was the popular name for the steamers which crossed the Tay?

41. What street used to be Dundee's main street? The Murraygate, the Seagate, or the Nethergate?

DUNDEE, WHITEHALL STREET 1878 SA000119
(Courtesy of University of St Andrews Library)

DUNDEE, THE COURT HOUSE 1899 SA000122
(Courtesy of University of St Andrews Library)

42. Which pub has a model of the Town House above its doors?

43. What did Dundonians call the balconies at the back of their tenements?

44. Who was the 'wonder horse' who could be ridden in the City Arcades?

45. What did Dundee housewives commonly use to transport their laundry to the washhouse?

DUNDEE, HILL STREET SCHOOL c1900 SA000190
(Courtesy of University of St Andrews Library)

46. What did men who were known as 'kettle bilers' do?

DUNDEE, THE DOCKS FROM PROTECTION WALLS 1878 SA000148
(Courtesy of University of St Andrews Library)

DUNDEE, THE GREENMARKET 1888 SA000125
(Courtesy of University of St Andrews Library)

47. In which Dundee park can you find Dundee Zoo?

48. What is the name of the cathedral that can be seen at the head of the Seagate?

DUNDEE AND THE RIVER TAY 1938 SA000127
(Courtesy of University of St Andrews Library)

49. What did George Wishart do on Wishart Arch?

50. In which Lochee cinema was the game of bingo first played in Dundee?

DUNDEE, THE KING'S THEATRE c1909 SA000198
(Courtesy of University of St Andrews Library)

DUNDEE, THE CALEDONIAN RAILWAY STATION 1893

SA000168 (Courtesy of University of St Andrews Library)

DUNDEE QUIZ ANSWERS

1. 'Dundee' is thought to come from the Celtic 'Duntaw' (hill on the Tay), or possibly from the Iron Age fort which was located on the top of the Law and was called Dun Diagh.

2. The old name for the Hilltown.

3. In 1191 Dundee was granted burgh status by David, Earl of Huntingdon.

4. Henry VIII's.

5. The right to use the area of the Howff as a burial ground.

6. They all mysteriously sank in the Tay.

7. Bonnets.

8. A Humpback Whale.

9. The Theatre Royal in Castle Street - opened in 1800.

10. Jute, jam and journalism - the three industries that helped to build the city. The jute and jam industry have gone, and today only journalism survives within Dundee.

11. Sir G Gilbert Scott in 1867. It was known as 'the finest Albert Memorial outside London'.

12. 28 December 1879.

13. The Dundee & Newtyle railway line tunnel. The builders faced the particularly difficult problem of how to navigate the Law. Their solution was to create a quarter-mile-long tunnel through the eastern flank of the hill!

14. The 'Unicorn', built in 1824 and brought to Dundee in 1873.

15. James Chalmers. The postage stamp was first suggested by the Dundee bookseller in 1822. Chalmers's idea of cheap postage and adhesive slips as a means of franking letters was the basis of our present mailing system.

16. A witch, who was the last witch burnt to death in the city in November 1699. Local legend tells of a young man who left Dundee a poor sailor and returned the captain of a fine ship. On entering the Tay, he commented on the strange smell in the air, and was told that a witch was being burnt at the stake. On hearing her name, Grizzel Jaffrey, he ordered that the ship be turned around, and he never returned to Dundee. Grizzell Jaffrey was his mother.

17. A few months before the Wright Brothers, Preston Watson achieved powered flight in Dundee with his 'wiggle-waggle' flying machine.

18. In 1988 the High School played the part of the Berlin Reichstag in Dennis Potter's 'Christabel'.

19. They are better known as Dundee's Nine Incorporated Trades, which were formed in the 16th century.

20. On 11 May 1797 Admiral Duncan encountered the Dutch fleet off the coast near the village of Camperdown. The battle that followed lasted for five hours, but the Dutch eventually surrendered to Admiral Duncan.

21. Dundee's last execution by hanging was carried out on 24 April 1889. William Henry Bury strangled his wife, stabbed her viciously, and then kept her body in a box (which his friends unknowingly played cards upon) for several days before confessing to the crime.

22. Hidden behind later buildings on the High Street and accessed through Gray's Close, Gardyne's Land is the oldest residential building to survive in Dundee. The house was built for a prosperous merchant, and its sophistication is an indicator of Dundee's wealth and status at the time.

23. In July 1906, a fire destroyed Watson's whisky bond and caused much damage to the street. The Dundee Yearbook from the period states that the Seagate was turned into 'a river of burning whisky'!

24. The ship the 'Mars' was moored in the Tay from 1869 and was home to boys, many orphaned or delinquents, until it was broken up in 1929.

25. The Keillor family business began when a Mrs Keillor invented a new recipe for marmalade after receiving a batch of particularly bitter oranges. Her son, James, established the business, and the company began to produce jam as well as marmalade enjoyed all over the world.

26. In 1991 Dundee celebrated its octocentenary (800 years) with a year-long birthday party. Most memorable of the events was a summer carnival, and many remember the gasometer that was made to look like a giant birthday cake.

27. Dundee's time gun was situated in the grounds of Dudhope Castle high above the city. Normally fired daily at 1pm, it was silenced in 1916 so as not to disturb shell-shocked soldiers recovering in Dundee Royal Infirmary.

DUNDEE QUIZ ANSWERS

28. Winston Churchill was Liberal MP for Dundee from 1908 until his humiliating defeat in 1922, after which he vowed never to return to the city, a vow which he kept.

29. Desperate Dan from the Dandy.

30. Children made up a large part of Dundee's textile industries work force; many were employed as 'half-timers', spending part of the day working and part of the day in school. The half-time system was not abolished until as late as 1936.

31. In the archives at Dundee University, a piece of sailcloth from Nelson's Victory survives. The sails from important ships were often cut up to make souvenirs, but this piece is particularly interesting as it bears the maker's stamp, Baxter Bros from Dundee.

32. Tents or wagon covers. Jute canvas was used for tents and wagon covers, sacking for coal and grain, and for horses' nosebags, among many other products. Tents from Dundee could be found being used by the American and Australian gold diggers, and Dundee's jute tarpaulins covered the pioneer's wagons as they travelled throughout the United States. Money from Dundee helped to establish and build the railroads in the US, and Dundee jute merchants invested in cattle and ranching.

33. Whale oil.

34. Cox's Stack. Built in 1865, it is 280 feet high; it is still a prominent Lochee landmark, and one of the few mill chimneys still to be seen in Dundee.

35. The Wellcome Trust Biocentre.

36. The RRS 'Discovery'. Captain Scott, or 'Scott of the Antarctic', became a national hero when he completed his National Antarctic Expedition of 1901-04. Dundee shipbuilders built the RRS 'Discovery' especially for the expedition; through their experience of building whaling ships, they were able to provide Scott with a vessel that could withstand the demanding journey. Another Dundee ship, the RRS 'Terra Nova', was used for Scott's fateful second expedition to reach the South Pole in 1910.

37. Brian Cox was born in the city and first worked in Dundee Rep.

38. 572 feet.

39. Submarines. Dundee's harbour was an important submarine base during both conflicts, with French, Dutch, Norwegian and Russian vessels docking there.

40. The 'Fifies' provided a regular service across the Tay before the building of the Tay Road Bridge in 1966.

41. The Seagate. The Seagate was the most important street within the town; when Robert I granted a piece of land where a tolbooth could be built in 1325, it was probably situated at the Seagate end of Peter Street. The market cross was also at first situated in the Seagate. The site is still marked today with a cross pattern built into the cobbles at the bottom of Peter Street.

42. The Pillars on Crichton Street.

43. 'Pletties'.

44. Champion was a coin-operated children's ride, well known to several generation of Dundee's children. It is now housed in the McManus Galleries.

45. A pram!

46. They were husbands who stayed at home to look after the household chores and children while their wives worked (kettle-boilers).

47. Camperdown Park, so called after Admiral Duncan's victory.

48. St Paul's Cathedral.

49. Preach. The Wishart Arch still stands in the Cowgate today, although the surrounding buildings have disappeared. The arch was said to have been used by the reformer George Wishart to preach to the townsfolk within the city walls and the plague victims outwith them.

50. The Rialto in August 1961. The Rialto Bingo & Social Club held bingo games every Saturday night. The Rialto still operated as a cinema in case the game wasn't popular!

GOUDHURST, MEASURING THE HOPS 1904 52571

GENERAL HISTORY QUIZ QUESTIONS

1. Which 20th-century Prime Minister was a proficient bricklayer and a member of the union?

2. In Victorian times, what powerful substance did many fashionable society ladies use to spice up their afternoon tea parties?

3. What was the first battle of the English Civil War on 23 October 1642?

4. Who was Queen Victoria's first Prime Minister?

5. Which Michigan-born dentist was arrested in Canada for the murder of his wife in London?

6. For what crime was Titus Oates pilloried in the stocks and flogged every year?

7. What crime was committed by Burke and Hare?

8. What language was Elizabeth I not fluent in? German, French, Latin, or Italian?

9. In 1834 six Dorset farm labourers were transported to Australia. By what name are these men usually known?

HORNING, ON THE BROADS 1902 48108

MARKET DRAYTON, MARKET DAY 1911 63338

10. At which battle was Richard III slain?

11. Who was the first Prime Minister to live at Chequers?

12. Who was the leader of the Women's Social and Political Union?

13. What year were women granted the vote on the Isle of Man?
1881, 1902, 1912, or 1946?

RHYL, DONKEYS ON THE SANDS 1891 29151

14. Which king signed the Magna Carta in 1215 at Runnymede?

15. In which city was the infamous Peterloo Massacre on 16 August 1819?

16. Who were the mother and father of Elizabeth I?

17. Before the French Revolution in 1789, who is reported to have said 'Let them eat cake'?

18. Who wore two shirts in which to be executed, and why?

19. Which queen was known as Bloody Mary?

20. Who was the only English pope?

21. Which British king married May of Teck?

22. At the outbreak of World War I, who was the British Prime Minister?

23. What great structure, designed by Joseph Paxton, was built in 1851?

24. What were the names of the two princes believed to have been murdered in the Tower of London in 1483?

25. What unusual accident eventually caused the death of the Prince of Wales, eldest son of George II?

26. Which of Dickens's novels depicts the struggles and strife of factory workers in Victorian England?

EVERSLEY, THE WHITE HART 1906 57011

CASTLETON, SPEEDWELL CAVERN 1909 61785

27. How old was William Shakespeare when he got married? 24, 25, 19, or 18?

28. What crime occurred on 8 August 1963 that shocked public opinion in Britain?

29. Who had to hide in an oak tree to save his life after a military
    defeat?

30. After Henry VIII's Dissolution of the Monasteries, what are
some of the new owners of the monastery buildings rumoured
to have done with some of the illuminated manuscripts they
found?

KING'S LYNN, HIGH STREET 1908 60023

31. In July 1888, 1,500 female employees went on strike at a factory at Bow in East London. What did they manufacture?

32. Who was the Irish saint who legend says saw the Loch Ness Monster in Scotland?
St Columba, St Patrick, St Andrew, or St Aidan?

33. Which English woman made this prophecy:
'Carriages without horses shall go, And accidents fill the world with woe. Around the world thoughts shall fly, In the twinkling of an eye.'?

34. Which tax was levied between 1696 and 1851?

35. How long did the Hundred Years' War last? 116 years, 94 years, 100 years, or 108 years?

36. Who was called the 'Old Pretender'?

37. In 1629 William Harvey published the details of a discovery he had made. What was it?

38. Put these wars and battles in the order in which they took place:
    A. The Battle of Agincourt
    B. The Battle of Hastings
    C. Marston Moor
    D. Wars of the Roses

39. In British army slang, what was a 'dead man'?

40. When was the Poll Tax first introduced in England?

CLOVELLY, POST OFFICE, TRANSFER OF MAIL 1936 87551

41. Who was the first Prime Minister of Britain?

42. What is pannage?

43. What were the Welshmen of the Rebecca Riots, who dressed up as women, protesting against?

44. How many people did the 1715 Riot Act have to be read to, in order for them to be guilty of a felony, and liable to the punishment of death? 6, 12, 27, or 250?

CHALFORD, THE VILLAGE 1910 62713

45. What was the joint stock company, the South Sea Company, set up in 1711 to trade in?

46. In the Middle Ages, a split stick was used by royal officials to record sums of money paid. Notches were cut on it representing payments. What was it called?

EASTBOURNE, THE PIER 1925 77946

WEYMOUTH, THE SANDS 1909 61597

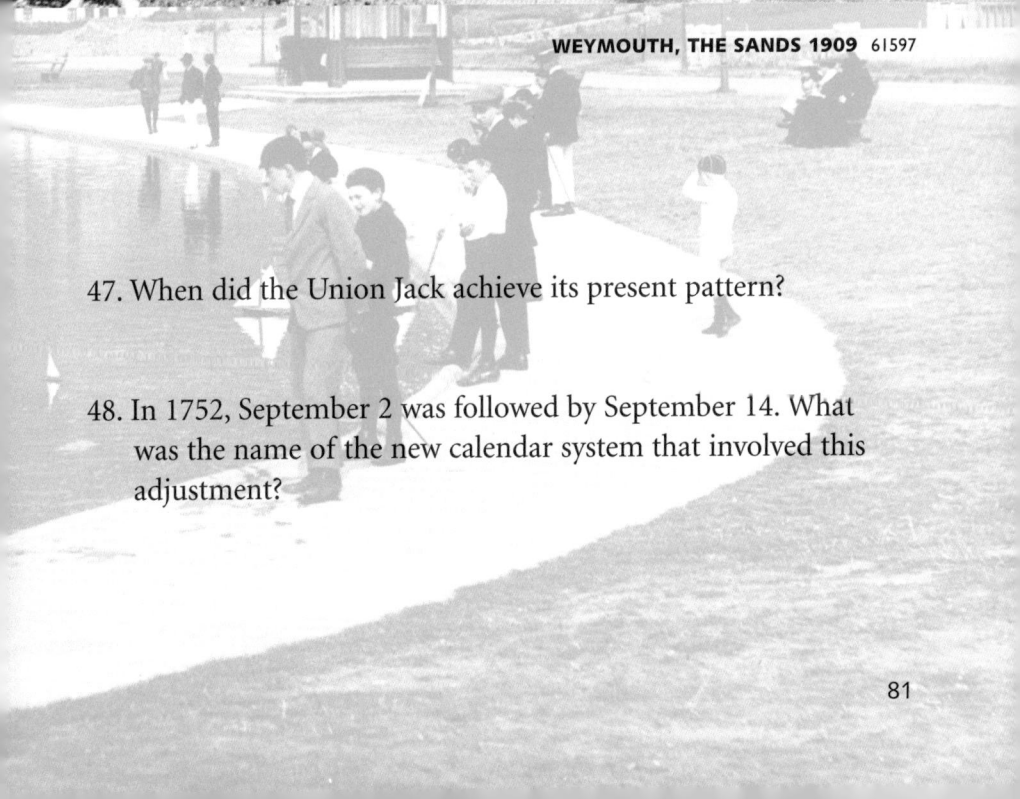

47. When did the Union Jack achieve its present pattern?

48. In 1752, September 2 was followed by September 14. What was the name of the new calendar system that involved this adjustment?

NEWBY BRIDGE, THE SWAN HOTEL 1914 67414

49. Coffee houses were patronised by literary giants such as Dryden, Johnson, and Pope. How many coffee houses were there in London in the 18th century?
10, 50, 250, or 1800?

50. Who was the first British Prime Minister to live at 10 Downing Street?

TENBY 1890 28091

GENERAL HISTORY QUIZ ANSWERS

1. Winston Churchill.

2. Opium.

3. Edgehill.

4. Lord Melbourne.

5. Dr Crippen. He buried her body in the basement of his London house.

6. For giving false evidence against Catholics.

7. They murdered people and sold their corpses to unscrupulous surgeons for dissection.

8. German.

9. The Tolpuddle Martyrs.

10. The Battle of Bosworth Field.

11. Lloyd George.

12. Emmeline Pankhurst.

13. 1881.

14. King John.

15. Manchester.

16. Henry VIII and Anne Boleyn.

17. Marie Antoinette.

18. Charles I. The weather was cold and he did not want to be seen shivering.

19. Mary I, the daughter of Henry VIII and Catherine of Aragon. She married Philip II of Spain, and was a devout Catholic. She earned her nickname from her persecution of Protestants.

20. Adrian IV, born Nicholas Brakespeare in 1100.

21. George V (she was known in this country as Mary).

22. Herbert Asquith.

23. The Crystal Palace.

24. Edward V and his brother Richard Duke of York, the sons of Edward IV.

25. He was hit on the head by a cricket ball.

GENERAL HISTORY QUIZ ANSWERS

26. 'Hard Times', published in 1854.

27. 18.

28. The Great Train Robbery.

29. Charles II.

30. They used them as lavatory paper.

31. Matches. They worked at the Bryant and May factory.

32. St Columba, born cAD521.

33. Mother Shipton, born in Norfolk in 1485.

34. Window Tax, which was payable on a house with more than six windows.

35. 116 years, between 1337 and 1453.

36. James III (the son of James II). In 1715 he gathered together a force of 10,000 men and invaded England. The Jacobites fought their way as far as Preston, where they were dispersed.

37. The circulation of the blood. He was physician extraordinary to James I.

38. B (1066) A (1415) D (1455-85) C (1644).

39. An empty bottle.

40. In 1222, on every person over the age of 14.

41. Robert Walpole. As first Lord of the Treasury between 1721 and 1742 he presided over the cabinet.

42. The right of tenants to graze their swine in the woods of a manor.

43. They destroyed turnpike houses, being unhappy about the levels of tolls.

44. 12.

45. Slaves in Latin America.

46. A tally.

47. In 1801, when the cross of St Patrick was added to the crosses of St George and St Andrew.

48. The Gregorian Calendar.

49. 1800.

50. Sir Robert Walpole (1676-1745).

Ottakar's Bookshops

Ottakar's bookshops, the first of which opened in Brighton in 1988, can now be found in over 130 towns and cities across the United Kingdom. Expansion was gradual throughout the 1990s, but the chain has expanded rapidly in recent years, with many new shop openings and the acquisition of shops from James Thin and Hammicks.

Ottakar's has always known that a shop's local profile is as important, if not more important, than the chain's national profile, and has encouraged its staff to make their shops a part of the local community, tailoring stock to suit the area and forging links with local schools and businesses.

Local history has always been a strong area for Ottakar's, and the company has published its own award winning local history titles, based on text written by its customers, in recent years.

With a reputation for friendly, intelligent and enthusiastic booksellers, warm, inviting shops with an excellent range of books and related products, Ottakar's is now one of the UK's most popular booksellers. In 2003 and then again in 2004 it won the prestigious Best Bookselling Company of the Year Award at the British Book Awards.

Ottakar's has commissioned The Francis Frith Collection to create a series of town history books similar to this volume, as well as a range of stylish gift products, all illustrated with historical photographs.

Participating Ottakar's bookshops can be found in the following towns and cities:

Aberdeen	Fareham	Ormskirk
Abergavenny	Farnham	Petersfield
Aberystwyth	Folkestone	Portsmouth
Andover	Glasgow	Poole
Ashford	Gloucester	Redhill
Ayr	Greenwich	St Albans
Banbury	Grimsby	St Andrews
Barnstaple	Guildford	St Neots
Basildon	Harrogate	St Helier
Berkhamsted	Hastings	Salisbury
Bishop's Stortford	Haywards Heath	Sheffield
Boston	Hemel Hempstead	Stafford
Brentwood	High Wycombe	Staines
Bromley	Horsham	Stevenage
Bury St Edmunds	Huddersfield	Sutton Coldfield
Camberley	Inverness	Teddington
Canterbury	Isle of Wight	Tenterden
Carmarthen	Kendal	Tiverton
Chatham	King's Lynn	Torquay
Chelmsford	Kirkcaldy	Trowbridge
Cheltenham	Lancaster	Truro
Cirencester	Lincoln	Tunbridge Wells
Coventry	Llandudno	Twickenham
Crawley	Loughborough	Walsall
Darlington	Lowestoft	Wilmslow and
Dorchester	Luton	Alderley Edge
Douglas, Isle of Man	Lymington	Wells
Dumfries	Maidenhead	Weston-super-Mare
Dundee	Maidstone	Windsor
East Grinstead	Market Harborough	Witney
Eastbourne	Milton Keynes	Woking
Elgin	Newport	Worcester
Enfield	Newton Abbot	Yeovil
Epsom	Norwich	
Falkirk	Oban	

Francis Frith
Pioneer Victorian Photographer

Francis Frith, founder of the world-famous photographic archive, was a complex and multi-talented man. A devout Quaker and a highly successful Victorian businessman, he was philosophical by nature and pioneering in outlook. By 1855 he had already established a wholesale grocery business in Liverpool, and sold it for the astonishing sum of £200,000, which is the equivalent today of over £15,000,000. Now in his thirties, and captivated by the new science of photography, Frith set out on a series of pioneering journeys up the Nile and to the Near East.

INTRIGUE AND EXPLORATION

He was the first photographer to venture beyond the sixth cataract of the Nile. Africa was still the mysterious 'Dark Continent', and Stanley and Livingstone's historic meeting was a decade into the future. The conditions for picture taking confound belief. He laboured for hours in his wicker dark-room in the sweltering heat of the desert, while the volatile chemicals fizzed dangerously in their trays. Back in London he exhibited his photographs and was 'rapturously cheered' by members of the Royal Society. His reputation as a photographer was made overnight.

VENTURE OF A LIFE-TIME

By the 1870s the railways had threaded their way across the country, and Bank Holidays and half-day Saturdays had been made obligatory by Act of Parliament. All of a sudden the working man and his family were able to enjoy days out, take holidays, and see a little more of the world.

With typical business acumen, Francis Frith foresaw that these new tourists would enjoy having souvenirs to commemorate their days out. For the next thirty years he travelled the country by train and by pony and trap, producing fine photographs of seaside resorts and beauty spots that were keenly bought by millions of Victorians. These prints were painstakingly pasted into family albums and pored over during the dark nights of winter, rekindling precious memories of summer excursions. Frith's studio was soon supplying retail shops all over the country, and by 1890 F Frith & Co had become the greatest specialist photographic publishing company in the world, with over 2,000 sales outlets, and pioneered the picture postcard.

FRANCIS FRITH'S LEGACY

Francis Frith had died in 1898 at his villa in Cannes, his great project still growing. By 1970 the archive he created contained over a third of a million pictures showing 7,000 British towns and villages.

Frith's legacy to us today is of immense significance and value, for the magnificent archive of evocative photographs he created provides a unique record of change in the cities, towns and villages throughout Britain over a century and more. Frith and his fellow studio photographers revisited locations many times down the years to update their views, compiling for us an enthralling and colourful pageant of British life and character.

We are fortunate that Frith was dedicated to recording the minutiae of everyday life. For it is this sheer wealth of visual data, the painstaking chronicle of changes in dress, transport, street layouts, buildings, housing and landscape that captivates us so much today, offering us a powerful link with the past and with the lives of our ancestors.

Computers have now made it possible for Frith's many thousands of images to be accessed almost instantly. The archive offers every one of us an opportunity to examine the places where we and our families have lived and worked down the years. Its images, depicting our shared past, are now bringing pleasure and enlightenment to millions around the world a century and more after his death.

For further information visit: www.francisfrith.co.uk